STEREOTYPES AND SLANG:

A SURVEY OF NATIONAL STEREOTYPING IN ENGLISH SLANG

Christian Peer

Christian Peer

STEREOTYPES AND SLANG

A Survey of National Stereotyping in English Slang

ibidem-Verlag
Stuttgart

Bibliografische Information Der Deutschen Bibliothek

Die Deutsche Bibliothek verzeichnet diese Publikation in der Deutschen Nationalbibliografie; detaillierte bibliografische Daten sind im Internet über <http://dnb.ddb.de> abrufbar.

∞
Gedruckt auf alterungsbeständigem, säurefreien Papier
Printed on acid-free paper

ISBN-10: 3-89821-715-9
ISBN-13: 978-3-89821-715-6

© *ibidem*-Verlag
Stuttgart 2006
Alle Rechte vorbehalten

Das Werk einschließlich aller seiner Teile ist urheberrechtlich geschützt. Jede Verwertung außerhalb der engen Grenzen des Urheberrechtsgesetzes ist ohne Zustimmung des Verlages unzulässig und strafbar. Dies gilt insbesondere für Vervielfältigungen, Übersetzungen, Mikroverfilmungen und elektronische Speicherformen sowie die Einspeicherung und Verarbeitung in elektronischen Systemen.

Printed in Germany

to my mum and my dad.
thank you for everything – you are really great!

CONTENTS

1 INTRODUCTION 11

2 STEREOTYPES AND STEREOTYPING 13
2.1 Theoretical Preliminaries 13
2.1.1 The Origin of the Term Stereotype 13
2.1.2 Lippmann's Concept of Stereotypes 14
2.1.3 Definition and Characteristics of Stereotypes 15
2.1.4 The Cognitive Approach to Stereotypes 16
2.1.4.1 The Resistance of Stereotypes to Change 16
2.1.5 Stereotypes and Culture 17
2.2 Stereotypes and Language 19
2.2.1 The Transmission of Stereotypes Through Language 19
2.2.2 The Maintenance of Stereotypes Through Language 21
2.2.2.1 The Linguistic Intergroup Bias 21
2.3 Stereotypes in Linguistics 23
2.3.1 Zybatow's Classification of Linguistic Stereotypes 23
2.3.1.1 Assoziationsstereotypen 24
2.4 Summary 25

3 NATIONAL STEREOTYPES 27
3.1 The Definition of Nation 29
3.2 The Relation Between National Stereotypes and National
    Identity 31
3.3 The Functions of National Stereotypes 31
3.4 The Study by Katz and Braly 33
3.4.1 The Results 33
3.5 Summary 35

4 SLANG ... 35
4.1 The History and Origins of Slang ... 35
4.2 Towards a Definition of Slang ... 37
4.2.1 What Slang is: Proper Definitions ... 37
4.2.2 What Slang is Not: An Alternative Approach ... 37
4.2.2.1 Slang is Not Colloquial ... 38
4.2.2.2 Slang is Not Dialect ... 38
4.2.2.3 Slang is Not Jargon ... 38
4.2.2.4 Slang is Not Argot ... 39
4.2.2.5 Slang is Not Cant ... 39
4.2.2.6 Slang is Not Taboo ... 39
4.3 The Position of Slang Within the English Vocabulary ... 41
4.4 The Characteristics of Slang ... 43
4.4.1 Slang is a Question of Vocabulary ... 43
4.4.2 Slang is Found in Spoken Language ... 43
4.4.3 Slang is Found in Informal Situations ... 44
4.4.4 Slang is a Relative Concept ... 44
4.4.5 Slang is Constantly Changing ... 45
4.4.6 Slang is Creative ... 45
4.5 How Slang Terms Enter the Language ... 47
4.6 The Usage of Slang: Linguistic Situations ... 47
4.7 The Functions of Slang ... 49
4.8 Slang – A Poetry of Its Own ... 51
4.8.1 Figurative Devices in Slang ... 52
4.9 Summary ... 55

5 ANALYSIS OF SLANG TERMS ... 57
5.1 Explanation of the Method Applied in the Analysis ... 59
5.2 Slang Terms Containing French Stereotypes ... 61

5.2.1 General Analysis 69
5.3 Slang Terms Containing Irish Stereotypes 71
5.3.1 General Analysis 80
5.4 Slang Terms Containing Dutch Stereotypes 81
5.4.1 General Analysis 86
5.5 Slang Terms Containing Jewish Stereotypes 87
5.5.1 General Analysis 92
5.6 Slang Terms Containing German Stereotypes 93
5.6.1 General Analysis 95
5.7 Slang Terms Containing English Stereotypes 95
5.7.1 General Analysis 99

6 CONCLUSION 101

7 BIBLIOGRAPHY 103

1 INTRODUCTION

The theoretical basis of this paper is the assumption that stereotyping is a phenomenon which manifests itself primarily through language. It is further based on the observation that slang, being a particular part of the English vocabulary, provides a large number of expressions that imply stereotypes.

The paper's topic focus lies on investigating the nature of stereotyping and slang, illustrating the subject by a survey that analyses which national stereotypes are contained in selected slang terms, and how those stereotypes are expressed.

To make a comprehensive understanding of the subject possible, the paper starts with the theoretical preliminaries to the field of stereotypes and stereotyping. An emphasis is put on the interrelation between stereotypes and language. Thus, the concept of stereotypes in linguistics is taken into consideration as well. The paper then deals with the phenomenon of national stereotyping in particular. The next part provides a comprehensive overview of the field of slang, since slang is the linguistic medium for stereotyping that this paper concentrates on. The emphasis here lies on investigating the unique nature and poetic aspects of slang that are particularly significant for the paper's subject.

The survey in the last chapter has two central focuses. First, it investigates the content of national stereotypes contained in certain slang terms. Second, it points out how slang works as a linguistic means to convey those stereotypes. Thus, consideration is given to the figurative and semantic aspects of the expressions selected. The overall aim of the survey is to illustrate and apply the theoretical contents that are discussed and worked out in the course of the paper.

2 STEREOTYPES AND STEREOTYPING

Stereotyping involves judging people as members of certain categories or groups rather than individuals. Thus, a key feature of stereotyping is to ignore the variability within a group of people. For example, we tend to assign certain characteristics to the individual members of a particular national group just because they are English or French or whatever. Though we hear people in the media saying that stereotyping is wrong and that we should try to stop it, everyone of us has stereotypes about 'the others' and this will quite certainly always be the case.

The following chapters are designed to provide the basic information about the history of stereotypes, what stereotypes exactly are, how stereotyping works and why people do it. Furthermore it is explained in which way culture and especially language relate to stereotypes and stereotyping. Finally the concept of stereotypes in linguistics is discussed as this is essential for the analysis of the dictionary entries in Chapter 5. The aim is to give the reader the necessary background knowledge for a comprehensive treatment of this paper's topic focus.

2.1 Theoretical Preliminaries

2.1.1 The Origin of the Term Stereotype

The roots of the term stereotype and its meaning lie in the world of printing. The word stereotype was invented by the French engraver and printer Firmin Didot and derives form the Greek words *stereos*, meaning 'solid' and *typos*, meaning 'model' or 'mark'. It originally referred to a "duplicate impression of an original typographical element used for printing instead of the original" (Wikipedia).

Over time, the word became a metaphor for any set of ideas repeated identically and en masse. The term cliché is also linked with the term stereotype. They both originally were printers' words and were used synonymously in their literal meanings. "Specifically, cliché was an onomatopoetic word for the sound that was made during the stereotyping process when the matrix hit molten metal" (Wikipedia).

2.1.2 Lippmann's Concept of Stereotypes

The study of stereotyping within the social sciences began with the publication of the book *Public Opinion* by the American journalist Walter Lippmann in 1922. According to Lippmann, stereotypes are simplified "pictures in our head" of people and events in the world (Lippmann, p. 27). He argues that the real world is much too complex for the human mind to be dealt with in every single aspect and that therefore our thinking and actions were mostly based on simplified pictures:

> There is economy in this. For the attempt to see all things freshly and in detail, rather than as types or generalities, is exhausting and among busy affairs practically out of the question. (Lippmann, p. 59)

Lippmann also emphasises the importance of one's culture for stereotypes and the process of stereotyping:

> In the great blooming, buzzing confusion of the outer world we pick out what our culture has already defined for us, and we tend to perceive that which we have picked out in the form stereotyped for us by our culture. (Lippmann, p. 81)

He furthermore claims that the content of stereotypes is largely incorrect and resistant to change. As it becomes evident in the following, Lippmann did already come up with the most important characteristics of stereotypes that are still topical in the social sciences today.

2.1.3 Definition and Characteristics of Stereotypes

There are many definitions in modern scientific literature of what stereotypes exactly are. Each one tries to emphasise a particular aspect of the phenomenon and it would be impossible to discuss them all in this paper. The following definition was taken from the online lexicon *Wikipedia* and was chosen for its briefness and clarity:

> In modern usage, a stereotype is a simplified mental picture of an individual or group of people who share certain characteristic (or stereotypical) qualities. The term is often used in a negative sense, and stereotypes are seen by many as undesirable beliefs which can be altered through education and/or familiarisation. (Wikipedia)

Although this definition is far from covering all aspects, it serves the purpose of providing the basis for the understanding of the following chapters. The communication scientist Martin Löschmann has provided seven key characteristics of stereotypes that are mentioned here to supplement the definition above:

1) (Über)Generalisierung [...]
2) Bezogenheit auf Personengruppen
3) [...] stabiler und starrer Character
4) meist negative [...] Bewertung
5) Einheit von kognitivem und emotionalem Charakter
6) Inkorrektheit, Rigidität und Irrationalität
7) Wirken im Unterbewußtsein. (Löschmann, p. 14)

In Chapter 5 it is demonstrated that all these characteristics can be identified through the analysis of the dictionary entries.

In his book *Stereotypes, Cognition and Culture* the psychologist Perry Hinton has worked out three important components of the process of stereotyping that shall be mentioned here to round off the basics. First, Hinton argues, "a group of people are identified by a specific characteristic" (Hinton, p. 7). By a specific characteristic Hinton means for instance nationality, gender or age. Second, a "set of additional [stereotypical] characteristics" is attributed to "the group as a whole" (Hinton, p. 7). For instance, English people are said to be reserved while Italians are said to be outgoing. Third, Hinton concludes, "on identifying a person as having the identifying meaningful characteristic [nationality, gender et cetera] we then attribute the stereotypical characteristic to them" (Hinton, p. 8).

2.1.4 The Cognitive Approach to Stereotypes

This chapter is designed to shed light on the cognitive aspects of stereotypes and stereotyping. It is explained in which way our cognitive system works and why stereotyping is practically inevitable.

The first thing that has to be considered is that our thinking is not always logical and systematic because it would simply take too much time and effort. That is why we often rely on so-called "heuristic" or "role-of-thumb strateg[ies]" (Hinton, p. 63). These include "automatic processing that is fast and relies on practised responses" (Hinton, p. 79). The problem is that this kind of thinking is very inflexible and sometimes, as in the case of stereotyping, simply illogical. The point here is that stereotypes have to be considered as a form of heuristic thinking. We do not regard people as the individuals they are but we categorise them. According to the linguist Lakoff, "[t]here is nothing more basic than categorization to our thought, perception, action and speech" (quoted in Hinton, p. 31). The reason for categorising is quite simple: We have a limited mental capacity. Hamilton and Troiler argue that we have to act in this way to prevent "cognitive overload" (Hamilton and Trolier, p. 76).

Though stereotyping is generally viewed as something negative, we have to be aware of the fact that everyone does it and has to do it, because it is so fundamental to our thinking.

2.1.4.1 The Resistance of Stereotypes to Change

In Chapter 2.1.3 the resistance to change has been mentioned as a basic characteristic of stereotypes. This phenomenon can be explained in connection with our cognitive system.

Psychologists have termed the process that forms the basis for maintaining stereotypes a self-fulfilling prophesy. The way it works is quite simple: Let us assume that someone employs the stereotype that Irish people are quarrelsome and aggressive. This person then spends his holidays somewhere in Ireland and witnesses a fight in the streets between two locals. It is quite safe to assume that this experience will confirm his stereotype although he could have witnessed the same scene in any other country. The decisive point is that people seek out "confirming information rather than disconfirming information" to test their beliefs (Hinton, p. 99).

Various studies have shown that national stereotypes have a particularly rigid and stable character. One of these studies is discussed later in this paper.

2.1.5 Stereotypes and Culture

Culture has an enormous impact on stereotypes and stereotyping. Various scientists have criticised the cognitive approach to stereotypes for neglecting the role of culture. According to the linguist Anna Wierzbicka, it is "impossible for a human being to study anything [...] from a totally extra-cultural point of view" (quoted in Stroinska, p. 42). Since national stereotypes can be understood as stereotypes shared between the members of a particular culture it is necessary to briefly discuss this relation here.

Lippmann, whose views were discussed in Chapter 2.1.2, already argued that "stereotypes are given by the culture as well as made by the person" (Hinton, p. 151). What Lippmann suggests is that stereotypes are part of our common knowledge, the knowledge that is shared and transmitted within a particular culture. Thus, most of the stereotypes people employ have to be considered as cultural stereotypes. In this connexion cultural stereotypes can be considered as social representations. According to the sociologist Serge Moscovici, a social representation is a "system of ideas, values and practises which provides individuals with a way of making sense of people and events in their social world [...]" (quoted in Hinton, p. 152). For instance, the Austrians employ the social representation and stereotype that

German people are industrious and striving. This is not the case because of individual observation but communication among Austrian people concerning the Germans. Nevertheless people internalise these social representations and by that they become personal stereotypes. The interdependence between personal and cultural stereotypes (or social representations) is illustrated by figure 1.

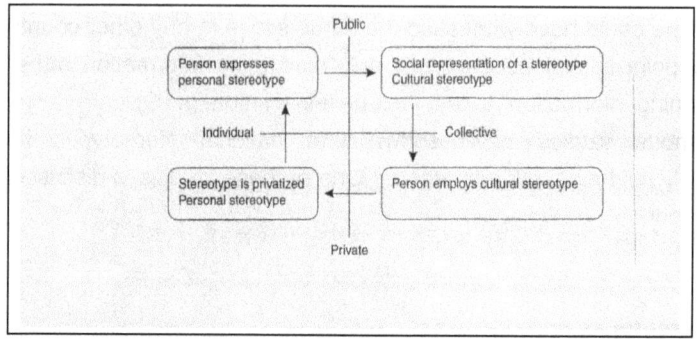

Figure 1 (Hinton, p. 146)

The 'problem' is that people believe the stereotyped views (social representations) that have been transmitted by their culture to be the only correct way of viewing the world after having internalised them. The psychologist Robert Brown called this phenomenon "cultural absolutism or ethnocentrism of stereotypes" (Brown, p. 117). People tend to view their culture and nation (called *in-group* in psychological jargon) more positive than other cultures and nations (*out-groups*). Out-groups are normally stereotyped in a negative manner. That is the reason why the content of stereotypes of other nations, especially that one found in slang terms, is almost exclusively negative as it is demonstrated in Chapter 5.

2.2 Stereotypes and Language

Since the topic focus of this paper is to study both how and which national stereotypes are expressed in slang terms it is necessary to investigate the relation between stereotypes and language. This chapter gives an overview of how language functions both to transmit and maintain stereotypes.

In the last two or three decades there has been a growing interest among scientists from different disciplines to study stereotypes and stereotyping by investigating certain aspects of language rather than to focus on cognitive aspects. The linguist Uta Quasthoff was one of the first to put an emphasis on the linguistic aspects of stereotypes. In her book *Soziales Vorurteil und Kommunikation - eine sprachwissenschaftliche Analyse des Stereotyps* she states:

> Ich gehe also davon aus, daß es sich beim Phänomen des Stereotyps in erster Linie um eine sozialpsychologische Erscheinung handelt, die sich jedoch sprachlich manifestiert und in sehr enger Beziehung zur sprachlichen Äußerung steht. (Quasthoff, p. 13)

Quasthoff introduced a very important point that is of great importance for the topic focus of this paper: Stereotypes are essentially linguistic behaviour. Or as Hinton argues: "We can only observe stereotypes through their linguistic expression" (Hinton, p. 25). Considering this fact it seems evident that language must also be the dominant means to communicate and transmit stereotypes among members of a particular culture. This point is discussed in the next chapter.

2.2.1 The Transmission of Stereotypes Through Language

Our language is full of stereotypes although we are principally not aware of this. The fact is that most stereotypes have been internalised and are thus manifested on a subconscious level as it has already been suggested in Chapter 2.1.3. Still it is possible to work out the content of stereotypic beliefs by analysing a particular aspect of the given language as for instance a part of its lexicon. This is done in Chapter 5 and it will become evident that slang provides a perfect field for analysing stereotypes within language.

The psychologist and linguist Anne Maas argues that "[o]n the most general level, culturally shared beliefs are wired into the vocabulary of a given language" (Maas 1996, p. 194). Stereotypes are culturally shared beliefs and thus can be found in lexical terms. It has been mentioned earlier in this paper that stereotypes are emotionally loaded mental representations. Thus, it must be assumed that also the lexical terms that imply them have a heavy 'emotional baggage'. Slang being a part of vocabulary that is highly emotive is therefore the perfect field for stereotyping as it is proven later in this paper.

If children are confronted with lexical terms that imply stereotypic beliefs it is safe to say that they will internalise and employ these beliefs over the years. The following example illustrates this: An Austrian can refer to German people by either using the neutral term *Germans* or the derogative term *Piefke*. Both expressions denote the same people. But while the first is neutral in its connotation, the second one implies the negative stereotype of Germans that quite many Austrians have. So if a child is repeatedly confronted with the latter term it will acquire the negative stereotype. Another example would be the names that were given to homosexuals in English speaking countries. Homosexuals used to be called either *queers* or *fags*. Both were derogative slang terms with a negative connotation. Homosexuals introduced the slang term *gay* which due to its actual meaning has a positive connotation and by now has largely replaced *queer* and *fag* (Maas 1996, p. 199). This illustrates roughly how stereotypic beliefs are transmitted interpersonally and on a more general level from one generation to the next.

Another important aspect is the role of the mass media and popular culture. They both provide powerful means for the communication and also formation of stereotypes. On the one hand the mass media and the internet in particular speeded up the flow of information enormously. Arguing on the basis of the cognitive approach that was discussed in Chapter 2.1.4, it could be suggested that the enormous amount of information we have to process

everyday makes stereotyping more necessary than ever simply to avoid a cognitive overload. On the other hand it has to be considered that stereotypes have always been part of popular culture and entertainment. Plays and soap operas often employ so-called stock characters such as the villain, the romantic lover, the hot-
blooded Italian or the reserved English gentleman just to name a few.

2.2.2 The Maintenance of Stereotypes Through Language

Language functions in a subtle way not only to transmit but also to maintain stereotypes as it is shown in this chapter.

It has already been discussed in Chapter 2.1.5 that people tend to assess their in-group more positive in every respect than the out-group. But so far this point has only been discussed from the cognitive point of view. Maas introduced a linguistic model called "Linguistic Intergroup Bias" (Maas 1996, p. 209) that investigates how language abstraction is used to maintain stereotypic beliefs.

2.2.2.1 The Linguistic Intergroup Bias

According to the Linguistic Intergroup Bias model, specific positive in-group and negative out-group behavioural episodes tend to be described in relatively abstract lexical terms. The opposite is the case if the behaviour is judged as negative. It then tends to be described in relatively concrete terms (Maas 1996, p. 209). Maas suggests four levels of language abstraction:
1) Descriptive action verbs which are the most concrete terms such as 'hit' in the sentence 'Peter hit Paul'.
2) The slightly more abstract interpretative action verbs as in 'Peter hurt Paul'.
3) State verbs represent the third level such as 'Peter hates Paul'.
4) The most abstract terms are adjectives as in 'Peter is aggressive'. They describe no longer a specific behaviour but a general characteristic of the person. (Maas 1996, p. 210)
The idea behind it is illustrated by the following example:

An English football fan employs the stereotype that Irish people are quarrelsome. After a football match there has been a fight between English and Irish fans which this person has witnessed. It is quite likely that he will use a statement somehow similar to the following to refer to the fight (or behavioural episode): 'It's always the same with these aggressive, pugnacious Irish fans'. Not only does he express his national stereotype of Irish people by saying this but he also confirms it in terms of language abstraction.

2.3 Stereotypes in Linguistics

This chapter provides a brief overview of how stereotypes are viewed in linguistics. The main focus is put on the classification of linguistic stereotypes introduced by Lew Zybatow.

The concept of the stereotype was introduced in linguistics by the language philosopher Hilary Putnam in the 1970s. Putnam argues that the understanding of stereotypes belongs to our common language knowledge and that they are tied to the use of particular expressions. He defines a stereotype as "eine konventionell verwurzelte, häufig übelmeinende und möglicherweise völlig aus der Luft gegriffene Meinung darüber, wie ein X aussehe, was es tue oder was es sei" (Putnam, p. 68). Quasthoff, who frequently refers to Putnam in her book, claims: "Ein Stereotyp ist der verbale Ausdruck einer auf soziale Gruppen oder einzelne Personen als deren Mitglieder gerichtete Überzeugung" (Quasthoff, p. 28). The decisive point is that stereotypes are tied to linguistic items. If these items are verbalised they evoke certain associations and connotations. Linguistic terms such as category labels (e.g. nationality, ethnicity, religious belief or political orientation) provide the necessary point of reference around which stereotypic information is organised. As a matter of fact, stereotyping would be impossible without
these "linguistic anchors" (Maas 1996, p. 196).

2.3.1 Zybatow's Classification of Linguistic Stereotypes

Lew Zybatow, professor at the Institut für Translationswissenschaft at the university of Innsbruck, has developed a classification of linguistic stereotypes that is particularly applicable to the analysis in Chapter 5.

Zybatow suggests that the concept of the linguistic stereotype is closely related to the meaning of stereotype defined by Lippmann which has already been discussed in Chapter 2.1.2. He identifies four types of linguistic stereotypes according to the way the mental content of the stereotype is related to the linguistic expression:
1) "Bedeutungsstereotypen" (Zyabtow, p. 21)

2) "Interpretationsstereotypen" (ibid.)
3) "Assoziationsstereotypen" (ibid.) and
4) "Abbildungsstereotypen" (ibid.)
The decisive one for the analysis of slang terms in this paper is number three.

2.3.1.1 Assoziationsstereotypen

Zybatow suggests that these stereotypes do not determine the semantic meaning of certain lexical items but are connected to them in an associative manner (Zybatow, pp. 52-53). This idea applies to the slang items that are analysed in this paper. The following example illustrates this: *French method* is a slang term that means oral sex. If someone uses this term in an utterance he primarily refers to the action of fellatio. The important point is that the adjective *French* in this compound subconsciously or even consciously evokes a derogative stereotype of French people as being sexually queer, although the term may have been used in a 'neutral' context and the speaker had no intention to employ the particular national stereotype. The stereotype has a merely associative relation to the lexical item.

2.4 Summary

Chapter 2 provided the theoretical preliminaries to the field of stereotypes and stereotyping. Furthermore the cognitive, the cultural and the linguistic approach to stereotypes have been discussed to give the reader a more complex overview that is necessary for a comprehensive understanding of this paper's topic focus. A particular emphasis has been put on the role of language and the linguistic aspects of stereotypes and stereotyping due to the topic focus of this paper.

3 NATIONAL STEREOTYPES

Figure 2 (Walas, front cover)
[the labels on the drawers have been added by the author of this paper]

The image that has been chosen as an opening to this chapter particularly well visualises what is subsequently discussed. This chapter investigates the phenomenon of national stereotypes, discuss its relevance for one's national identity and presents some results from a study on national stereotypes.

In 1945 George Orwell wrote an essay with the title *Notes on Nationalism*. He explains, that by nationalism he means "the habit of assuming that human beings can be classified like insects and that the whole blocks of millions or tens of millions of people can be confidently labelled 'good' or 'bad'" (Orwell, p. 362). Orwell refers to the human tendency to categorise that has already been discussed in Chapter 2.1.4 and is elementary for stereotyping. He also emphasis how illogical and absurd this process actually is:

> [N]ations, and even vaguer entities such as the Catholic Church or the proletariat, are commonly thought of as individuals and often referred to as 'she'. Patently absurd remarks such as 'Germany is naturally treacherous' are to be found in any newspaper one opens, and reckless generalisations about national character ('The Spaniard is a natural aristocrat' or 'Every English-man is a hypocrite') are uttered bay almost everyone. Intermittently these generalisations are seen unfounded, but the habit of making them persists. (Orwell, p. 362)

Orwell wrote his essay within the historical context of World War II and he considered the human habit to categorise as dangerous, having just witnessed the terrible events in Nazi Germany. He thought it to be the foundation of fanaticism and authoritarian systems.

Orwell mentions two important concepts that have to be defined in this chapter. The one of *nation* and the one of *national character* which is closely linked to the idea of *national identity*.

3.1 The Definition of Nation

The following text, taken from the online lexicon *Wikipedia* is only a part of the whole definition that is provided by the source but it contains an important aspect:

> [...] The idea of a "nation" gained wide acceptance and popularity in the eighteenth century, when romantic nationalism was developed and used to shatter the old world order of dynastic or imperial hegemony. [...] The idea of a nation [still] remains somewhat vague, in that there is generally no strict definition for exactly who is considered to be a member of any particular nation. Many modern states show a great diversity of cultural behaviours and ethnic backgrounds. England may furnish a classic example: a territory which is not a state, since it has no government of its own, and which has large immigrant populations and diverse cultural behaviour, yet the English are often described as a nation. (Wikipedia)

It is stated that the idea of a nation is still indistinct today and this claim is well illustrated by the example of England. Considering this it becomes even more obvious how illogical the habit of national stereotyping actually is as there is not even a clear concept of what is being stereotyped. However, Anthony D. Smith, one of most important contemporary scholars of nationalism, provides a definition of *nation* that at least brings up the most important aspects behind the concept. According to him, a nation is "a named human population sharing a historical territory, [...] a mass, standardized public culture, a common economy and territorial mobility, and common legal rights and duties for all members of the collectivity" (quoted in Walas, p. 19). This definition emphasises the profound role of culture for the concept of a nation. The importance of culture for commonly held stereotypes has already been discussed in Chapter 2.1.5. The next chapter discusses the decisive aspects that have been brought up by the two definitions.

3.2 The Relation Between National Stereotypes and National Identity

Culture provides individuals with a *national identity*. One's national identity always contains a self-image of one's nation and stereotypes of others. The self-image in this context can be regarded as a kind of 'auto-stereotype'. That means it points out the way people see themselves and what is maybe even more important the way they would like to be seen by others. Berting and Villain-Gandossi argue that "[t]he concept of national identity is dependent on national stereotypes" (Walas, p. 19). It is suggested that national stereotypes help to form and articulate ones national identity by pointing out the (alleged) differences between the members of one's own nation and those others. For instance, Austrians tend to see themselves as 'gemütlich' in contrast to Germans whom they regard as laborious and striving and thus often stressed out. Berting and Villain-Gassondi also observe that "they [national stereotypes] often may be slumbering, to be brought back to daily life under certain circumstances" (Walas, p. 24). Such circumstances are for instance among countless other ones international football matches and periods of mass tourism. The latter is perfectly parodied in the Austrian TV-series *Die Piefke Saga*.

The decisive point here is that it has been shown that without stereotypes of others (especially national stereotypes) a positive and distinct image of one's own nation and its members could not exist. This phenomenon is also closely related to that of people favouring their in-group as it has been discussed in Chapter 2.1.5.

3.3 The Functions of National Stereotypes

Berting and Villain-Gassondi have suggested the following functions of national stereotypes that are mentioned here to round off the main focus of Chapter 3 before discussing a study on national stereotypes:

1. They provide the members of a community with ready-made, shared frames of reference which enable them to structure […] the outside world, the other people.
2. They contribute to the cohesion among the members of a political community as they accentuate the sense of belongingness […].
3. They articulate the common values of a community by contrasting our values and habits with "the other".
4. They may be used to accentuate in a positive way that "our" collectivity is different from others […].
5. They may be used for inclusion and exclusion of persons and groups which are considered as having values and habits which are a menace to "our" values […]. (Walas, p. 23)

3.4 The Study by Katz and Braly

Ethnic and national stereotyping has been studied most in psychological research along with gender stereotyping (Hinton, p. 92). This circumstance can certainly be interpreted as a sign for the importance and social relevance of the topic. One of the first studies on the topic has been carried out by Katz and Braly in 1933 (Katz and Braly). This study was chosen by the author because it is easy to overview and its results are largely still topical today after more than seventy years. Most notably they are supposed to provide a possibility of comparison for the analysis in
Chapter 5.

The study was set up in the following way: One hundred students from the University of Princeton were given a so-called trait checklist. It contained eighty-four descriptive adjectives such as industrious, conservative, intelligent and materialistic. Then they were asked to chose those adjectives that in their opinion best described ten ethnic groups. If they wanted to use an adjective that was not on the list they could do so. The ethnic groups were ten nationalities, among them Jews, Irish, English, Chinese and Germans. Finally they had to chose the five most characteristic adjectives for each nationality and do a preferential ranking.

3.4.1 The Results

The key result was that there was a "high degree of consensus between the participants in the study as to the characteristic of the group, indicating a common stereotype" (Hinton, p. 10). Subsequent studies have proven that many stereotypical traits were chosen over a long period of time (ibid.). This can be interpreted as evidence for the resistance of national stereotypes to change.

Unfortunately only four nationalities from this study are among the ones being discussed in the slang term analysis in Chapter 5.
In the following the five adjectives most frequently assigned to each nationality are given:

ENGLISH
Sportsmanlike............53%
Intelligent..................46%
Conventional..............34%
Tradition-loving...........31%
Conservative..............30%

IRISH
Pugnacious................45%
Quick-tempered..........39%
Witty..........................38%
Honest.......................32%
Very religious.............29%

GERMANS
Scientifically-minded............78%
Industrious...........................65%
Stolid....................................44%
Intelligent.............................32%
Methodical...........................31%

JEWS
Shrewd................................79%
Mercenary...........................49%
Industrious..........................48%
Grasping.............................34%
Intelligent............................29%

(quoted in Sodi and Bergius, pp. 22-23)

These results are then referred to in Chapter 5.

3.5 Summary

Chapter 3 investigated the concept of national stereotypes, their relation to the notion of national identity as well as their functions. It furthermore discussed different aspects of the concept of nation and introduced a study on national stereotypes and some of its results.

4 SLANG

This chapter is designed to give the reader a comprehensive overview of the field of slang. An emphasis is put on those aspects that are relevant for the analysis of the particular slang terms in Chapter 5.

4.1 The History and Origins of Slang

The origin of the word *slang* is uncertain. Maybe it derived from *sling* or is "a clipping that combines elements in such phrases as *beggars' language* or *rogues' language*" (*OCEL*, p. 940). Originally the term *slang* was used by British criminals in the 16th century to refer to their own special language. They shaped it in such a way that it was incomprehensible to outsiders who referred to the language by the term *cant*. It was at first believed to be foreign and scholars thought that it had either originated in Romania or had a relationship to French. By the end of the 16th century this new style of speaking was considered to be a language "without reason or order" (Thorne, p. 23). During the 18th century schoolmasters taught their pupils that cant, which by this time had developed into slang for its usage was not restricted to the criminal underworld anymore, was not the correct usage of English. Slang was then considered to be taboo and the negative attitude towards slang lingered. The English belletrist J.P. Thomas wrote in 1825: "The language of slang is the conversation of fools. Men of discretion will not pervert language to unprofitable purposes of conversational mimicry" (quoted in Partridge, p. 7). In 1828, Noah Webster, who was the first lexicographer who entered the word *slang* in a standard dictionary, defined it as "low, vulgar unmeaning language" (quoted in Lighter, p. 227). However, slang slowly started to escape the harsh criticism of being associated with criminals. Society was developing a new attitude towards slang and by the early 1920's slang had gained the interest of popular writers. This happened because "the 1914-18 war caused more slang to come into being than any other time in the history of English. As the regiments, squadrons and battalions came together from all over the English-speaking world, they brought their informal language with them. The effect was explosively generative" (Burchfield, p. 135). Slang flourished from then onwards especially among the so-called subcultures who searched for a way to express their identity. Jazz terms, surfing slang, words used by beatniks, hippies, drug addicts, blacks, rockers and mods entered the English language and popular culture in particular. Today slang is still one of the most important fields for the creation of new words and meanings.

4.2 Towards a Definition of Slang

Quite frequently it is not easy to draw an exact line between slang, dialect expressions or colloquialisms for instance. Thus, many authors find it difficult to exactly define what slang is and suggest an alternative approach to the question. However, there are some quite useful and clear definitions to be found in literature on slang. These will be given first in this paper. Then an alternative approach is considered.

4.2.1 What Slang is: Proper Definitions

A fairly vague definition is given by Katamba in his book *English Words*: "Slang is the term used to describe a variety of language with informal, often faddy, non-standard vocabulary" (Katamba, p. 169). The one provided by the *OED* is already somewhat more precise: "[L]anguage of a highly colloquial type, considered as below the level of educated standard speech, and consisting of new words or current words employed in some special sense." What is interesting is that both of the just mentioned definitions define slang as a kind of language although slang is almost exclusively found in vocabulary and not in grammar or syntactical choices. This important point is discussed later in Chapter 4.4.1. The best available definition that was found by the author of this paper is given by Lighter: "Slang denotes an informal, non-standard, nontechnical vocabulary composed chiefly of novel-sounding synonyms (and near synonyms) for standard words and phrases; [...]" (Lighter, p. 220).

4.2.2 What Slang is Not: An Alternative Approach

The linguist Paul Roberts said that slang was "one of those things that everybody can recognize and nobody can define" (quoted in Anderson and T., p. 69). The *OCEL* observes that "slang must be distinguished from [...] other subsets of the lexicon as [...] dialect words, jargon, [...] colloquialisms, cant and argot [...]" (*OECL,* p. 940). What this chapter does is trying to suggest what slang is by defining that what it is not.

4.2.2.1 Slang is Not Colloquial

The term *colloquial* denotes an informal, everyday speech. As Burgess states that "[c]olloquialisms are informal expressions not to be used in elevated discourse" (Burgess 1993, p. 260). Although slang terms are informal expressions too, there is an important difference to consider. Lighter puts it the following:

> Whereas the merely informal or colloquial imparts a natural, unstilted tone to discourse, slang is conspicuously divergent, taking the place of words that lie near the familiar core of standard English. The aim and chief function of slang is to lower and disavow the dignity of discourse. (Lighter, p. 221)

This important aspect is considered again in Chapter 4.6.

4.2.2.2 Slang is Not Dialect

It has already been mentioned that slang is almost solely a question of vocabulary. This is not the case with dialect. As Stockwell observes, "dialect covers word choices, syntactic ordering and all the other grammatical choices a speaker could make" (Stockwell, p. 5). Dialect is furthermore to a particular region or social class. Slang does not necessarily have to be that.

4.2.2.3 Slang is Not Jargon

Jargon usually denotes "specialist vocabularies associated with 'occupations' that people engage in" (Jackson, p. 128). The term is often used pejoratively by 'outsiders' to whom the particular jargon of a group is incomprehensible. This usually the case if specialists such as doctors or lawyers use their jargon in an inappropriate context. The negative connotation of term is also reflected in its etymology: "[...] from late Middle English forms *iargo(u)n, gargoun, girgoun* the twittering and chattering of birds, meaningless talk, gibberish, from Old French *jargoun, gargon, gergon"* (*OCEL,* p.543).

4.2.2.4 Slang is Not Argot

Argot is the term that denotes the language of "a restricted, often suspect, social group" (*OCEL,* p. 81). Burgess observes that "argots usually originate in tightly closed cliques, in groups where there is a strong sense of camaraderie and highly developed group solidarity based primarily on community of occupation" (Burgess 1993, p. 264). Slang on the contrary is in principle accessible to the whole language community and can often be found in the media and pop culture. The following excerpt from Anthony Burgess' book *A Clockwork Orange* is a famous example for argot: "Our pockets were full of deng, so there was no real need from the point of view of crasting any more pretty polly to tolchock some old veck in an alley and viddy him swim in his blood [...]" (Burgess 1998, p. 17).

4.2.2.5 Slang is Not Cant

Although the meaning of the term *slang* originally derived from cant, the word (cant) is still used as a term for the language of criminals. "Thus", Anderson and Trudgill state, "slang has, a concept, moved a long way from its origin" (Anderson and T., p. 78).

4.2.2.6 Slang is Not Taboo

According to *The Concise Oxford Dictionary, taboo* is "a prohibition or restriction imposed on certain behaviour, word usage, etc. by social custom". Though slang is not regarded as 'good' language by quite many people, they however would not label it taboo. Jackson observes that "in lexicology, the label *taboo* is usually applied to words that would be extremely offensive if spoken in most contexts" (Jackson, p. 140). *Cunt,* for instance, is such a word. Slang provides an enormous amount of metaphors for the word that are not considered to be taboo but sometimes rather have a comical effect: "apple, bacon sandwich, [...] butcher's window, canyon, [...] chopped liver,

[…] Dead End Street, […] front bum, fur burger, […] garden of Eden, golden doughnut […]" (Burgess 1993, p. 263).

4.3 The Position of Slang Within the English Vocabulary

Quite a lot of the entries in a dictionary are marked with certain labels such as formal, informal, colloquial, technical or slang for example. This indicates that these words are restricted in their use in contrast to 'common' Standard English words. Such words belong to a number of special sub-sets of the English vocabulary.

The *OED* provides the following diagram (Figure 3) in the "General Explanations" at the beginning. It displays the editors' concept of the structure of the English vocabulary.

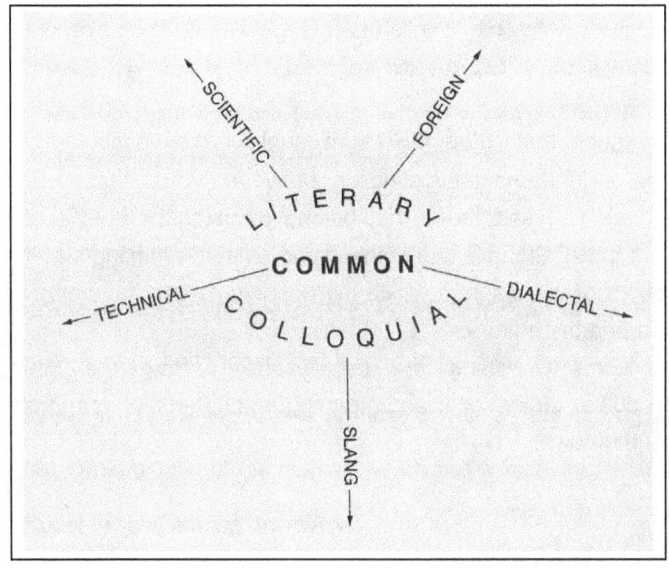

Figure 3 (*OED*, p. xxiv)

The explanatory note to the diagram runs as follows:

> The above diagram will explain itself, as an attempt to express to the eye the aspect in which the vocabulary is here presented, and also some of the relations of its elements typical and aberrant. The

centre is occupied by the 'common' words, in which literary and colloquial usage meet. 'Scientific' and 'foreign' words enter the common language mainly through literature; 'slang' words ascend through colloquial use; the 'technical' terms of crafts and processes, and the 'dialect' words, blend with the common language both in speech and literature. Slang also touches on one side the technical terminology of trades and occupations, as in 'nautical slang', 'Public School slang', 'the slang of the Stock Exchange', and on another passes into true dialect. Dialects similarly pass into foreign languages. Scientific terminology passes on one side into purely foreign words, on another it blends with the technical vocabulary of art and manufactures. It is not possible to fix the point at which the 'English Language' stops, along any of these diverging lines. (*OED,* p. xxiv)

Jackson argues that "[t]he *OED's* account of the vocabulary of English recognizes a fundamental distinction between words that belong to the common core [...] and those that belong to particular specialist sub-sets" (Jackson, p. 119). Slang is one of these sub-sets. It is striking that it is located at the bottom of the diagram which might imply its general status or at least the one among the editors.

The words of slang are usually taken from the common core. However, due to their specialised meaning and context of usage they form a sub-set of their own.

4.4 The Characteristics of Slang

So far, it has been tried to define slang and place it within the English vocabulary. This chapter discusses the question what slang is like and what makes it 'special' compared to Standard English.

4.4.1 Slang is a Question of Vocabulary

As it has already been mentioned, slang is almost exclusively found in words and not in grammatical or syntactical choices. Anderson and Trudgill state that "[t]here are perhaps a handful of features which could be regarded as typical of slang grammar, but there are very few compared to the enormous number of words belonging to slang" (Anderson and T., p. 73).

4.4.2 Slang is Found in Spoken Language

According to the OECL, "[s]lang belongs to the spoken part of language" (OECL, p. 940). This appears to be obvious since most situations in which people talk are less formal than those in which they write. Slang is below the colloquial level and thus it is very unlikely to find it in documents, official letters or newspapers. However, slang can be found in certain novels, short stories and the like, especially in the dialogues. Still slang gains its life and freshness by being used in informal conversations and contexts. Anderson and Trudgill provide the following example: "If you go and watch a football game, you will no doubt hear a lot of slang from the crowd around you. The next morning when you read about the match in the newspaper, there will be far less slang in the papers' coverage of the game, we promise you" (Anderson and T., p. 72).

4.4.3 Slang is Found in Informal Situations

The formality of language is tied to the situation as it is discussed more extensively in Chapter 4.6. Slang is informal and its usage lowers the formality of discourse. According to Lighter, "it [slang] is found in contexts where standard English is not cultivated: work environments, military and naval bases, high school and college campuses, prisons, sporting arenas, neighbourhood taverns, and locations for leisure-time activities" (Lighter, p. 221). This is an important aspect as far as stereotyping is concerned. Since stereotyping is considered to be against political correctness, it is unlikely to find slang expressions that imply national stereotypes in radio reports or television programmes by the BBC for instance.

4.4.4 Slang is a Relative Concept

One thing that makes it so difficult to exactly define slang is the fact that what is slang for one person must not necessarily be slang for another. Slang is relative. The following example illustrates this:

> *Lad* and *lass* may be slang for some speakers of English. For others they are simply neutral, plain language and nothing else. In the North of England, *lad* is a neutral stylistic expression […]. However, in the south *lad* is a slang term, as in *He's one of the lads* meaning 'He is one of the gang' […]. (Anderson and T., p. 70)

This phenomenon can also be observed in dictionaries. For instance, *fag* (meaning 'cigarette') is labelled *slang* in *The Concise Oxford Dictionary* and only *informal* in *The Collins German Dictionary*. That circumstance suggests that there exists no general agreement among lexicographers which words have to be labelled slang and which not.

4.4.5 Slang is Constantly Changing

Slang changes through time. In fact, slang might probably be the very sub-set of the English vocabulary within which the most changes happen. As Anderson and Trudgill observe, "[i]t would be very unusual for a slang word to live on in the language for a thousand years or more. If it does, it will probably not be slang all the time" (Anderson and T., p. 85). Most slang terms are local in time. Old slang words are constantly replaced by the enormous amount of new ones that continually enter the language. Still there exist some exceptions. *Bones,* for instance, as a slang word meaning 'dice' was already used by Geoffrey Chaucer in the 14th century and is still slang (*OECL,* p. 941).

However, the short-lived nature of slang constitutes a serious problem to lexicographers. It makes its recording extremely difficult. The *OECL* states that "current slang cannot be found in dictionaries, which are always engaged in catching up, and may never include certain terms, because they have proved to be highly ephemeral [...]" (*OECL,* p. 942)
Thus, the slang terms analysed in this paper can only represent a small part of all the expressions implying national stereotypes that exist.

4.4.6 Slang is Creative

The creative aspect of slang is certainly the most striking one. People use slang to keep their language fresh, amusing, interesting, startling and sometimes even shocking. Slang, as it is discussed later in Chapter 4.7, has a lot in common with poetry. It highlights more than any other part of the English vocabulary the creativity of its users and the joy that lies in playing with language. The following example illustrates this. It is an excerpt from a list of one-hundred-twenty-five slang terms for 'stupid person' that was put together by fifty-five children aged between thirteen and fourteen.

[...] wally, dingo, dozy, duck, dodo, dumbo, Nelly, Johnny, gooseberry, featherbrain, dur brain, nappy rash, Scooby Doo, sausage, dappy, thicko, dopey, spaz, headcase, flop head, bumbreath, dimwit, banana head, spongecake, bird brain, burgerbrain, goofy, nitwit, numbskull, dozy, melon, dummy, Erny, silly willy, pillock, nutcase, pranny, kipper, dap, bowl head, smiffy, zombie, cauliflower, div, nutter, flid [...] (quoted in Anderson and T., pp. 88-89)

4.5 How Slang Terms Enter the Language

Most slang terms are created by 'recycling' words or parts of words that belong to the common core of the English vocabulary. Anderson and Trudgill suggest a circulation of words which is illustrated in the diagram (Figure 4) on the next page. By the term *vogue words* that occurs in the left box of the diagram they mean "words and phrases which become popular and very frequent for a short period of time" (Anderson and T., p. 81). Just like slang terms "they receive a wider meaning or function than the ordinary usage of word" (ibid.).

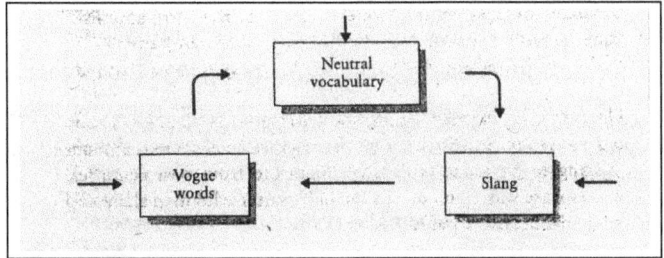

Figure 4 (Anderson and T., p. 82)

Another source of slang terms is the invention of new words. *Goof* meaning 'to blunder' or *freak out* meaning 'to lose control' are such examples. The third way is by borrowing words from another language as *gazlon,* for instance, that derives from Yiddish and means 'swindler'. However, by far most slang terms come into being by changing the meaning of 'ordinary' words.

4.6 The Usage of Slang: Linguistic Situations

A linguistic situation is the context in which a discourse takes place. The kind of linguistic situation depends on a variety of factors. Meyer provides a compact overview of such factors in his book *Synchronic English Linguistics*:

> [The kind of linguistic situation depends on]
> - the speaker's and hearer's social position or social orientation
> - the speaker's and the hearer's relationship with each other (close / less close)
>   - the kind of situation (formal / less formal)
>   - the individual speaker's linguistic skill and flexibility
>   - the hearer's tolerance (Meyer, p. 164)

It has already been discussed that the formality of language is tied to the situation. For instance, the language used between close friends is most certainly less formal than that between a university professor and one of his students. The usage of slang, with slang being a rather informal kind of vocabulary, is thus restricted to particular linguistic situations depending on their formal context. A continuum of the degree of formality could be seen as follows, with *taboo* being the least formal level:

official – formal – neutral – informal – colloquial – slang – taboo.

The following example illustrates how the same meaning is expressed on each level of formality:
- 'The consumption of nutriments is prohibited in this establishment' (official)
- 'You are requested not to consume food in this establishment!' (formal)
- 'Eating is not allowed here' (neutral)
- 'Please don't eat here' (informal)
- 'You can't feed your face here' (colloquial)
- 'Lay off the nosh' (slang)
- 'Lay off the fucking nosh' (taboo)

4.7 The Functions of Slang

Employing slang is usually a consciously made linguistic choice. That means, the speaker has certain intentions and the slang he uses fulfils one or more particular functions.

There are various such functions or reasons for using slang mentioned in literature, but the probably best and most complex list of them is provided by the British lexicographer Eric Partridge, who wrote extensively about slang, in his famous book *Slang Today and Yesterday*:

1. In sheer high spirits, by the young in heart as well as by the young in years; 'just for the fun of the thing'; in playfulness or waggishness.
2. As an exercise either in wit and ingenuity or in humour. (The motive behind this is usually self-display or snobbishness, emulation or responsiveness, delight in virtuosity).
3. To be 'different', to be novel.
4. To be picturesque (either positively or - as in the wish to avoid insipidity - negatively).
5. To be unmistakeably arresting, even startling.
6. To escape from clichés, or to be brief and concise. (Actuated by impatience with existing terms.)
7. To enrich the language. (This deliberateness is rare save among the well-educated, Cockneys forming the most notable exception; it is literary rather than spontaneous.)
8. To lend an air of solidity, concreteness, to the abstract; of earthiness to the idealistic; of immediacy and appositeness to the remote. (In the cultured the effort is usually premeditated, while in the uncultured it is almost always unconscious when it is not rather subconscious.)
9a. To lesson the sting of, or on the other hand to give additional point to, a refusal, a rejection, a recantation;
9b. To reduce, perhaps also to disperse, the solemnity, the pomposity, the excessive seriousness of a conversation (or of a piece of writing);

9c. To soften the tragedy, to lighten or to 'prettify' the inevitability of death or madness, or to mask the ugliness or the pity of profound turpitude (e.g. treachery, ingratitude); and/or thus to enable the speaker or his auditor or both to endure, to 'carry on'.

10. To speak or write down to an inferior, or to amuse a superior public; or merely to be on a colloquial level with either one's audience or one's subject matter.

11. For ease of social intercourse. (Not to be confused or merged with the preceding.)

12. To induce either friendliness or intimacy of a deep or a durable kind. (Same remark.)

13. To show that one belongs to a certain school, trade, or profession, artistic or intellectual set, or social class; in brief, to be 'in the swim' or to establish contact.

14. Hence, to show or prove that someone is not 'in the swim'.

15. To be secret - not understood by those around one. (Children, students, lovers, members of political secret societies, and criminals in or out of prison, innocent persons in prison, are the chief exponents.) (Partridge, pp. 6-7)

These functions sum up and cover practically everything what has been stated about the nature of slang so far in this paper.

Number 13 and its complement 14 in combination with number 10 are surely the most important functions as far as the phenomenon of stereotyping in slang is concerned. Crystal even suggests, that number 13 and 14 are "the primary functions of slang from Eric Partridge's list" (Crystal , p. 182). The decisive point is, that stereotyping is primarily about devaluing 'the others' and sanitising one's own image. Slang terms that convey (national) stereotypes are predominantly of a derogative nature and have a negative connotation as it is shown in Chapter 5.

4.8 Slang – A Poetry of Its Own

The fact that slang has a lot in common with poetic language is significant for the method of analysis applied in Chapter 5. For instance, slang employs many of the same figurative devices. Among other aspects, it is investigated which figurative devices are employed in the individual slang terms.

Slang is both emotively and rethorically very different from standard vocabulary. "In comparison with ordinary English", Lighter observes, "it might well be said that slang works at heightened intensity [...]" (Lighter, p. 224). Thus, several colourful and even enthusiastic characterisations of slang can be found in literature as the following examples demonstrate.

The American poet Carl Sandburg said: "Slang is language that rolls up its sleeves, spits on its hands, and goes back to work" (quoted in Anderson and T., p. 69). Samuel Ichiye Hayakawa, a psychologist and semanticist, called slang "the poetry of everyday life" (quoted in Lighter, 224). Gilbert Keith Chesterton, an English novelist, observes: "The one stream of poetry that is constantly flowing is slang. Every day some nameless poet weaves some fairy tracery of popular language. [...] All slang is metaphor, and all metaphor is poetry" (quoted in Anderson and T., p. 69). Even the great Walt Whitman claims that slang is "an attempt of common humanity to escape from bald literalism and express itself illimitably [which] in highest walks produces pets and poems [...]" (quoted in Lighter, p. 236). Anthony Burgess sums it up by stating that "[slang] fulfils a desire to make poetry" (Burgess 1993, p. 263). The primary function of poetry is most certainly to express emotions and feelings. That applies to slang too as has already been suggested in Chapter 4.7.

In the following the focus is put on how the said poetry in slang works. The *OECL* states that "slang [has] the tendency to name things indirectly and figuratively, especially through metaphor, metonymy and irony" (OECL, p. 942). The mentioned figurative devices frequently occur in the slang terms in Chapter 5. Although there are undoubtedly dozens of different devices to be found in slang, the most frequent and important one is metaphor. A lot of slang expressions are metaphorical in origin. Leisi and Mair state that "[die] Neigung zu drastischer Metaphorik im Slang eine große Rolle spielt" (Leisi and M., p. 183). The slang term *Irish bouquet*, for instance, which denotes 'any form of projectile, usually a stone or a brick', illustrates this claim quite well.

However, many slang expressions that are truly creative in the first place lose much of their originality, appeal and freshness through continuous usage. Anderson and Trudgill observe that "they turn into rather ordinary lexical items. They are then often called *frozen metaphors*" (Anderson and T., p. 85). The enormous creativity that lies in slang, however, constantly provides new and startling expressions.

4.8.1 Figurative Devices in Slang

This chapter provides a list in alphabetical order of those figurative devices that repeatedly occur in the slang terms analysed in this paper. The definitions have been established by consulting the *OECL* and the *Wikipedia* online lexicon, unless stated otherwise.

- *Allusion:*
  The implicit referencing of a related object or circumstance, which has occurred or existed in an external context.

- *Antiphrasis:*
  See *Irony*.

- *Burlesque Metaphor:*
  Something is satirised by in an exaggerated way by comparison.

- *Camouflage or Eclipsis:*
  An unpleasant or taboo meaning is concealed by a neutral word or phrase that is not necessarily euphemistic.

- *Dysphemism:*

1. An expression that has been deliberately degraded to have unpleasant or taboo connotations.
2. The use of negative or disparaging expressions to describe someone or something.

- *Euphemism:*
A relatively mild, comforting or vague expression that replaces one that is taboo, negative, offensive or too direct.
- *Irony or Antiphrasis:*
1. Words with an implication opposite to their usual meaning. Ironic devices can be humorous to mildly sarcastic.
2. A word or words used contradictory to their usual meaning (= Antiphrasis).

- *Metaphor:*
A figure of speech that achieves its effect through association, comparison and resemblance.

- *Metonymy:*
A figurative device that designates something by the name of something associated with it.

- *Personification:*
Animals, plants, elements of nature or abstract ideas are given human attributes.

- *Pun:*
A figure of speech which consists of a deliberate confusion of similar words or phrases for rhetorical effect, whether humorous or serious.

- *Sarcasm:*
The use of mockery, verbal taunts or bitter irony.

- *Schematismus:*

"Concealing a meaning by using figurative language, either out of necessity or for humour's sake" (*Silva Rhetoricae*).

4.9 Summary

Chapter 4 provided a comprehensive overview of the field of slang. First the origins of slang have been discussed, followed by the attempt to define slang. An alternative approach has also been considered by trying to define slang by what it is not. Next, slang has been positioned within the English vocabulary. The characteristics as well as the usage and functions of slang have been investigated in the subsequent chapters. The main focus was put on the poetic nature of slang at the end of Chapter 4. A list of figurative devices that repeatedly occur in the analysis in Chapter 5 has been provided in 4.7.1.

5 ANALYSIS OF SLANG TERMS

This chapter provides a survey of particular slang terms containing national stereotypes. The aim of the survey is to work out the common national stereotypes that are implied, and to demonstrate how the 'poetry' in slang works. Thus, it is tried to cover the semantic as well as the figurative aspect.

The terms that have been chosen for analysing cover the following nationalities: French, Irish, Dutch, Jewish, German and English. This choice is intended to be exemplary and can by no means meet the claim to be representative, due to the given length of this paper.

All slang terms, except but three, that occur in the following chapters are taken from *The Cassel's Dictionary of Slang* by Jonathon Green. This dictionary contains both by far the most entries and covers all the relevant ones listed in *The Dictionary of Contemporary Slang, Slang and Euphemism* and *The Oxford Dictionary of Modern Slang* which all serve as primary sources for this paper. The three terms that cannot be found in Green's book are listed in the "List of Common Phrases Based on Stereotypes" from the *Wikipedia* online lexicon. Furthermore, only those expressions are analysed that explicitly display the nationality they refer to. That means, the following slang terms are either compounds (e.g. *French leave*) or verbs and adjectives that have been formed through conversion (e.g. *to dutch*) or derivation (e.g. *frenchified*). Conversion is the process "by which a word belonging to one word class is transferred to another word class without any concomitant change of form, either in pronunciation or spelling" (Jackson, p. 86). Derivation denotes the lexical process which "forms a new word out of an existing one by the addition of a derivational affix" (Jackson, p. 70). The reason for thus narrowing the choice, is that the following slang terms accessorily imply *Assoziationsstereotypen* in terms of Zybatow's classification of linguistic stereotypes, that has been discussed in Chapter 2.3.1.1. This is a decisive point concerning national stereotyping in language.

5.1 Explanation of the Method Applied in the Analysis

Each individual slang term is analysed regarding the following aspects: figurative device, semantic field, connotation and the content of the stereotype implied. The results for each term are listed by means of the chart pictured below:

slang term plus meaning
figurative device:
semantic field:
connotation:
content of stereotype implied[1]*:*

The occurring figurative devices, that are supposed to demonstrate how the 'poetry' in slang works, have been listed and explained in Chapter 4.7.1. The terms *semantic field* and *connotation* are yet to be defined:

• *Semantic Field:*
A group pattern or framework of related words that covers or reflects to an aspect of the world. The related words are grouped together on the basis of an element of shared meaning. Jackson, however, observes that "there is no set of agreed criteria for establishing semantic fields" (Jackson, p. 111).

• *Connotation:*
Connotation denotes the affective meaning of a word and refers to emotive and associational aspects of it. Connotation may be personal or common to a group. Connotations are thought to colour what a word 'really means' with emotion or value judgments.

The reason for suggesting a semantic field for each of the following slang terms is that the number of terms deriving from a particular semantic field (e.g. 'sexuality') within one nationality gives interesting clues on the common national stereotype. The connotation of each term, on the other

---
[1] abbr. as *fig.d., sem.f., conn.* and *con.st.i.* respectively in the following charts.

hand, is worth investigating as it has already been mentioned in various contexts before that stereotypes are 'emotionally loaded' concepts. Thus, the connotation of the expression hints at the emotional baggage of the implied stereotype.

Each group of slang terms referring to one particular nation is analysed in a separate chapter. A general analysis of the results from each group concludes the individual chapters.

5.2 Slang Terms Containing French Stereotypes

French 'bad language.'
fig.d.: sarcasm, metonymy.
sem.f.: language.
conn.: derogative.
con.st.i.: The French language is regarded as inferior to English. The French talk dirty.

French art 'fellatio.'
fig.d.: camouflage.
sem.f.: sexuality.
conn.: neutral.
con.st.i.: French art in its literal meaning is restricted to certain sexual practices.

French 'to fellate.'
fig.d.: camouflage.
sem.f.: sexuality.
conn.: negative.
con.st.i.: Oral sex generally used to be regarded as a French perversion. The French were seen as sexually perverted.

French aunt 'a flighty woman.'
fig.d.: euphemism.
sem.f.: derogative terms for women.
conn.: derogative.
con.st.i.: French women are flighty, careless.

French bath 'the use of perfumes as a deodorant in lieu of bathing.'
fig.d.: sarcasm.
sem.f.: bodily hygiene.
conn.: negative.
con.st.i.: The French are stereotyped as both physically and morally dirty. They try to 'conceal' this by using perfume.

French by injection 'said of anyone considered particularly well-versed in fellatio.'
fig.d.: sarcasm, schematismus.
sem.f.: sexuality.
conn.: derogative.
con.st.i.: The French are especially well-versed in fellatio.

French crown/ goods/ gout 'venereal disease.'
fig.d.: metaphor, schematismus.
sem.f.: diseases.
conn.: negative.
con.st.i.: France is the origin of venereal diseases and the French spread them.

French culture 'fellatio.'

fig.d.: antiphrasis.	
sem.f.: sexuality.	
conn.: neutral.	
con.st.i.: French culture in its literal meaning is restricted to particular sexual practices.	

French dip 'vaginal precoital fluid.'

fig.d.: schematismus.	
sem.f.: sexuality.	
conn.: sarcastic.	
con.st.i.: Everything in France, even food, is somehow in connection with sexuality. The French, who particularly enjoy having oral sex, 'eat' those bodily fluids.	

French disease 'venereal disease, esp. syphilis.'

fig.d.: metonymy.	
sem.f.: diseases.	
conn.: negative.	
con.st.i.: cf. *French crown.*	

French dressing 'semen.'

fig.d.: metaphor, camouflage.	
sem.f.: sexuality.	
conn.: sarcastic.	
con.st.i.: cf. *French dip.*	

French embassy 'any location, esp. a gym or YMCA, where homosexual activity is extensive and unchecked.'

fig.d.: allusion, irony.
sem.f.: sexuality.
conn.: slightly negative.
con.st.i.: The French have homosexual tendencies which they live out secretly in public locations.

Frencher 'one who enjoys oral sex, usu. a man.'

fig.d.: metonymy.
sem.f.: sexuality.
conn.: slightly negative.
con.st.i.: French men enjoy having oral sex. Oral sex is seen as something particularly French.

French-fried ice-cream 'semen.'

fig.d.: pun, metaphor.
sem.f.: sexuality.
conn.: sarcastic.
con.st.i.: cf. *French dip*.

French fries 'crack cocaine.'

fig.d.: metaphor.
sem.f.: drugs and narcotics.
conn.: negative.
con.st.i.: Everything that is morally condemnable is connected with France. Thus the French are corrupt people.

frenchie/ frenchy 1. 'a foolish man.'
2. 'a flighty woman.'

fig.d.: metonymy.	
sem.f.: 1. derogative terms for men. 2. derogative terms for women.	
conn.: derogative.	
con.st.i.: 1. Stupidity of the French. 2. cf. *French aunt*.	

frenchified 1. 'having venereal disease.'
2. 'usu. of a woman, sexually talented.'

fig.d.: metonymy.	
sem.f.: 1. diseases 2. sexuality.	
conn.: 1. negative. 2. derogative.	
con.st.i.: 1. cf. *French crown*. 2. French women are sexually talented.	

French inhale 'to blow out cigarette smoke through the nose.'

fig.d.: irony.	
sem.f.: semi-luxuries.	
conn.: derogative.	
con.st.i.: The French are sophisticated, conceited.	

French language expert 'a fellator.'
fig.d.: pun, irony.
sem.f.: sexuality.
conn.: derogative.
con.st.i.: The French are particularly well-versed in fellatio. The pun is on the French word *langue* which *language* originally derives from. *Langue* means 'language' as well as 'tongue'.

French language training 'teaching another person fellatio.'
fig.d.: pun, irony.
sem.f.: sexuality.
conn.: slightly negative.
con.st.i.: cf. *French language expert*.

French leave 'absenting oneself from a job or duty without prior permission.'
fig.d.: metonymy, sarcasm.
sem.f.: socially unwanted behaviour.
conn.: negative.
con.st.i.: The French are unreliable workers, employees.

French love 'fellatio.'
fig.d.: camouflage, metonymy.
sem.f.: sexuality.
conn.: neutral.
con.st.i.: Among the French sexuality is almost exclusively circled around fellatio.

French marbles 'venereal diseases, esp. syphilis.'

fig.d.:	metaphor.
sem.f.:	diseases.
conn.:	negative.
con.st.i.:	cf. *French crown.*

French measles/ cannibal 'venereal disease, esp. syphilis.'

fig.d.:	metonymy, dysphemism.
sem.f.:	diseases.
conn.:	negative.
con.st.i.:	cf. *French crown.*

French photographer 'a homosexual photographer.'

fig.d.:	metonymy.
sem.f.:	sexuality.
conn.:	derogative.
con.st.i.:	The French generally have homosexual tendencies.

French pig 'syphilis, esp. the syphilitic pustule or bubo.'

fig.d.:	dysphemism.
sem.f.:	diseases.
conn.:	negative.
con.st.i.:	cf. *French crown.*

French revolution 'the movement for homosexual rights.'

fig.d.: allusion, irony.
sem.f.: sexuality.
conn.: derogative.
con.st.i.: cf. *French photographer.* The importance of the actual French Revolution is deliberately played down.

French screwdriver 'a hammer.'

fig.d.: antiphrasis.
sem.f.: tools.
conn.: sarcastic.
con.st.i.: The French are too stupid and clumsy to use tools properly and perform simple manual tasks.

French stuff 1. 'pornography.'
2. 'any unusual sexual activity.'

fig.d.: camouflage, metonymy.
sem.f.: sexuality.
conn.: negative.
con.st.i.: The French are obsessed with unusual sexual practices and pornography.

French walk 'the posture assumed by those being thrown bodily out of a saloon.'

fig.d.: pun, sarcasm.
sem.f.: alcohol and drunkenness.
conn.: derogative.
con.st.i.: The pun is on *frog* which is a derogative term for a French person. The person thrown out by two others is held up with all four limbs spread out like a frog.

French wank 'the action of being masturbated between a woman's breasts.'
fig.d.: dysphemism.
sem.f.: sexuality.
conn.: negative.
con.st.i.: The French enjoy dirty, unusual sexual practices.

French way 'fellatio.'
fig.d.: metonymy, camouflage.
sem.f.: sexuality.
conn.: neutral.
con.st.i.: cf. *French*.

5.2.1 General Analysis

Unfortunately, the common stereotype of the French has not been investigated in the study by Katz and Braly that has been introduced in Chapter 3.4. However, according to the "List of Common Stereotypes based on Nationality, Ethnicity and Race" from the *Wikipedia* online lexicon, the stereotypical Frenchman has the following characteristics: "poor hygiene, smelly, nationally chauvinistic, [...] promiscuous, philanderers, adulterers, good cooks, [...] extremely rude - especially waiters, [...] smoke[s] far too much [...]" (*Wikipedia*). Interestingly, in this list only rather general and vague statements are made about the French's sexual habits. This is by no means the case with the slang terms. 18 out of a total of 32, which equals 56 percent, are from the semantic field of *sexuality*. The major part of those terms explicitly refers to fellatio. Burgess observes that "there is a tradition that this [oral sex] is a filthy Continental [and thus a French] habit" (Burgess 1993, p. 268). A key characteristic of slang is to work below the colloquial level and refer to things indirectly by the means of metaphor, metonymy and

camouflage, particularly when those things are socially taboo. It is thus not surprising that many slang expressions come from the field of sexuality. However, the fact that more than half the terms listed have a sexual meaning is striking. The key result here is that the stereotypical Frenchman is sex-obsessed, employs 'unusual and queer' sexual practices, has homosexual tendencies and is
morally dirty.

The second most entries, namely 6, which equals 19 percent come from the semantic field of (sexual) *diseases*. In the 17th and 18th century the stereotype of France being the origin of syphilis, which was by then widely spread in Britain, and the French spreading the disease was commonly employed among the English. This stereotype, however, is not current anymore.

5.3 Slang Terms Containing Irish Stereotypes

Irish it up 'put liquor into a beverage.' (*Wikipedia*)	
fig.d.: metonymy.	
sem.f.: alcohol and drunkenness.	
conn.: neutral.	
con.st.i.: The Irish drink a lot of alcohol. Drinking is a particularly Irish habit.	

get one's Irish up 'to lose one's temper.' (*Wikipedia*)	
fig.d.: metaphor.	
sem.f.: anger.	
conn.: slightly negative.	
con.st.i.: The Irish are quick-tempered and irascible.	

Irish ambulance 'a wheelbarrow.'	
fig.d.: metaphor.	
sem.f.: transportation.	
conn.: derogative.	
con.st.i.: The Irish are too poor and crude to transport sick people in a proper way.	

Irish apple 'a potato.'	
fig.d.: antiphrasis.	
sem.f.: food.	
conn.: ironic.	
con.st.i.: The Irish are obsessed with potatoes for it is the only food they have and can afford.	

Irish applesauce 'mashed potatoes.'

fig.d.:	antiphrasis, metaphor.
sem.f.:	food.
conn.:	ironic.
con.st.i.:	cf. *Irish apple*.

Irish apricot 'a potato.'

fig.d.:	antiphrasis.
sem.f.:	food.
conn.:	ironic.
con.st.i.:	The Irish are too stupid to tell an apricot from a potato. The only food Irish people know are potatoes. Alleged stupidity of the Irish.

Irish arms 'thick legs.'

fig.d.:	antiphrasis.
sem.f.:	appearance.
conn.:	derogative.
con.st.i.:	The Irish are stout and not well-built.

Irish baby buggy 'a wheelbarrow.'

fig.d.:	metaphor, sarcasm.
sem.f.:	transportation.
conn.:	sarcastic.
con.st.i.:	The Irish are too poor and crude to transport their babies in a proper way.

Irish beauty 'a woman with a pair of black eyes.'

fig.d.:	antiphrasis, sarcasm.
sem.f.:	physical violence.
conn.:	sarcastic.
con.st.i.:	Irish men are violent and beat their wives.

Irish bouquet 'any form of projectile, usu. a stone or brick.'

fig.d.:	metaphor, sarcasm.
sem.f.:	physical violence.
conn.:	negative.
con.st.i.:	The Irish are violent and pugnacious.

Irish by birth but Greek by injection 'a male homosexual.'

fig.d.:	metonymy, sarcasm.
sem.f.:	sexuality.
conn.:	derogative.
con.st.i.:	The Irish are particularly conservative in sexual practices. Catholic Irish people are allegedly very religious and thus regard homosexuality as a sin.

Irish caviar 'Irish stew.'

fig.d.:	irony.
sem.f.:	food.
conn.:	sarcastic.
con.st.i.:	The Irish are too poor to afford good quality food and have a lousy sense for it.

Irish channel 'the throat.'
fig.d.: metaphor.
sem.f.: alcohol and drunkenness.
conn.: negative.
con.st.i.: cf. *Irish it up.* Down the *Irish channel* flows alcohol.

Irish cherry 'a carrot.'
fig.d.: antiphrasis.
sem.f.: food.
conn.: ironic.
con.st.i.: cf. *Irish apricot.*

Irish chicken 'pork.'
fig.d.: irony.
sem.f.: food.
conn.: ironic.
con.st.i.: The Irish are too stupid to tell one kind of meat from the other because of their bad sense for food.

Irish clubhouse 'a police station.'
fig.d.: sarcasm.
sem.f.: crime.
conn.: negative.
con.st.i.: The Irish are criminal and most likely to be found at the police station.

Irish comics/ funnies 'the obituary columns in a newspaper.'

fig.d.: sarcasm.
sem.f.: print media.
conn.: sarcastic.
con.st.i.: Alleged illiteracy of the Irish.

Irish confetti 'bricks, esp. as thrown during riots.'

fig.d.: metaphor, sarcasm.
sem.f.: physical violence.
conn.: negative.
con.st.i.: cf. *Irish bouquet*. Irish people are constantly engaged in riots.

Irish dividend 'a non-existent or fictitious profit, a deficit, a stock assessment.'

fig.d.: antiphrasis.
sem.f.: money, business.
conn.: sarcastic.
con.st.i.: Poverty of the Irish. Irish people are bad businessmen.

Irish draperies 'cobwebs.'

fig.d.: metaphor, irony.
sem.f.: hygiene.
conn.: derogative.
con.st.i.: The Irish are untidy and dirty.

Irish flag 'a diaper, a nappy.'

fig.d.: metaphor, sarcasm.
sem.f.: hygiene.
conn.: derogative.
con.st.i.: Having many children, and thus large families, is something particularly Irish.

Irish fortune 'the vagina.'

fig.d.: metaphor.
sem.f.: sexuality.
conn.: derogative.
con.st.i.: The Irish's only fortune are their children which they have a lot of.

Irish grape 'a potato.'
fig.d.: antiphrasis.
sem.f.: food.
conn.: ironic.
con.st.i.: cf. *Irish apricot*.

Irish inch 'the erect penis.'

fig.d.: metonymy.
sem.f.: sexuality.
conn.: derogative.
con.st.i.: Irish men have small penises.

Irish kiss 'a head-butt.' (*Wikipedia*)
fig.d.: antiphrasis, sarcasm.
sem.f.: physical violence.
conn.: negative.
con.st.i.: The Irish are violent and quarrelsome.

Irish lace 'a spider's web.'
fig.d.: metaphor, irony.
sem.f.: hygiene.
conn.: derogative.
con.st.i.: cf. *Irish draperies*.

Irish legs 'heavy female legs.'
fig.d.: metonymy.
sem.f.: appearance.
conn.: derogative.
con.st.i.: Irish women are stout and thick-built.

Irishman's coat of arms 'two black eyes and a bleeding nose.'
fig.d.: metaphor, sarcasm.
sem.f.: physical violence.
conn.: sarcastic.
con.st.i.: cf. *Irish kiss*.

Irishman's dinner 'a fast.'
fig.d.: antiphrasis.
sem.f.: food
conn.: sarcastic.
con.st.i.: The Irish are too poor to afford anything to eat.

Irishman's necktie 'a rope.'
fig.d.: metaphor, irony.
sem.f.: clothing.
conn.: ironic.
con.st.i.: The Irish are too crude and poor to dress themselves properly.

Irishman's pocket 'a pocket that is both large and empty.'
fig.d.: metonymy, sarcasm.
sem.f.: money, business.
conn.: sarcastic.
con.st.i.: The Irish are poor and never have any money at hand.

Irishman's/ Irish sidewalk 'the street.'
fig.d.: antiphrasis.
sem.f.: -
conn.: ironic.
con.st.i.: The Irish are too stupid to tell the sidewalk from the street. Alleged stupidity of Irish people.

Irish promotion 'a cut in one's pay.'
fig.d.: antiphrasis, sarcasm.
sem.f.: money, business.
conn.: sarcastic.
con.st.i.: The Irish are bad employees.

Irish rose 'a stone, for throwing.'
fig.d.: metaphor, sarcasm.
sem.f.: physical violence.
conn.: negative.
con.st.i.: cf. *Irish bouquet.*

Irish screwdriver 'a hammer.'
fig.d.: antiphrasis.
sem.f.: tools.
conn.: sarcastic.
con.st.i.: The Irish are too stupid and clumsy to use tools properly and perform simple manual tasks. (cf. *French screwdriver.*)

Irish twins 'two siblings born within the same year, 9 to 12 months apart.'
fig.d.: metaphor, irony.
sem.f.: family.
conn.: derogative.
con.st.i.: cf. *Irish flag* and *Irish fortune.*

5.3.1 General Analysis

The two most frequently mentioned adjectives in Katz's and Braly's study to characterise the Irish are 'pugnacious' and 'quick-tempered' (cf. Chapter 3.4.1). 17 percent of the slang terms analysed are from the semantic field of *physical violence*. All those terms imply that the stereotypical Irishman is violent and short-tempered. As it can be seen, the common Irish stereotype in slang ties up with the one in Katz's and Braly's study.

The slang terms furthermore contain the stereotypes of the Irish being stupid (also illiterate), crude, addicted to potatoes, having many children and thus large families and drinking large quantities of alcohol. What is also striking, is the fact that all the mentioned expressions have exclusively negative or derogative connotations. Furthermore, irony and sarcasm are the most frequently occurring figurative devices that perfectly reinforce the stereotypes implied. Interestingly, the negative stereotype of the Irish is one of the most enduring national stereotypes among the English and Americans altogether.

5.4 Slang Terms Containing Dutch Stereotypes

dutch 1. 'to speak emphatically.'
2. 'to ruin another's business, social standing, enjoyment etc. with deliberate malice.'
3. 'to bet in such a way that the bank is broken.'

fig.d.: metonymy.
sem.f.: 1. communication. 2. and 3. money, business.
conn.: derogative.
con.st.i.: 1. The Dutch are bossy people. 2. and 3. The Dutch are malicious and unscrupulous businessmen.

Dutch auction 'a mock auction or sale in which the much-touted 'reductions' have no bearing in commercial fact.'

fig.d.: metonymy.
sem.f.: money, business.
conn.: negative.
con.st.i.: The Dutch are not to be trusted in business affairs.

Duch bargain 'a one-sided bargain.'

fig.d.: irony.
sem.f.: money, business.
conn.: ironic.
con.st.i.: cf. *Dutch auction*.

Dutch bath 'a very cursory wash.'

fig.d.:	irony.
sem.f.:	hygiene.
conn.:	derogative.
con.st.i.:	The Dutch are untidy, smelly and dirty.

Dutch build 'a stocky, thickset individual.'

fig.d.:	metonymy.
sem.f.:	appearance.
conn.:	derogative.
con.st.i.:	Dutch people are stocky and thickset.

Dutch concert/ medley 'any performance in which each musician plays a different tune; thus a general pejorative for a bad performance, musical or metaphorical.'

fig.d.:	irony.
sem.f.:	music.
conn.:	derogative.
con.st.i.:	The Dutch are bad musicians and performers.

Dutch courage 'cowardice that, fortified by generous quantities of alcohol, becomes (temporary) bravery.'

fig.d.:	antiphrasis.
sem.f.:	alcohol and drunkenness.
conn.:	negative.
con.st.i.:	The Dutch are naturally coward people and drink a lot of alcohol.

Dutch doggery 'a grog-shop.'
fig.d.: dysphemism.
sem.f.: alcohol and drunkenness.
conn.: negative.
con.st.i.: The Dutch are surly and consume a lot of alcohol.

Dutch fit 'a fit of temper.'
fig.d.: metonymy.
sem.f.: anger.
conn.: negative.
con.st.i.: The Dutch are irascible and quick-tempered.

Dutch foil/ gilding/ gold/ metal 'an alloy of 11 parts copper and 2 parts zinc, used as a substitute for gold leaf and presumably passed off as such to the unwary.'
fig.d.: metonymy.
sem.f.: money, business.
conn.: negative.
con.st.i.: Dutch businessmen are cheaters.

Dutch fuck 'the lighting of one cigarette form another, thus saving matches.'
fig.d.: dysphemism, metaphor.
sem.f.: meanness.
conn.: derogative.
con.st.i.: Dutch people are mean.

Dutch it 'to share expenses, usu. of a meal.'

fig.d.: metonymy.
sem.f.: meanness.
conn.: slightly negative.
con.st.i.: cf. *Dutch fuck.*

Dutch leave 'taking time off without permission, absenting oneself illegally.'

fig.d.: metonymy.
sem.f.: socially unwanted behaviour.
conn.: negative.
con.st.i.: The Dutch are unreliable workers, employees. (cf. *French leave*.)

Dutchman's cape 'a cloudbank at the horizon that gives the impression of being land.'

fig.d.: metaphor, irony.
sem.f.: celestial objects.
conn.: ironic.
con.st.i.: Dutch sailors are too stupid to tell a cloudbank from real land.

Dutchman's drink 'a drink that empties the pot or drains some form of communal drinking vessel.'

fig.d.: metonymy.
sem.f.: alcohol and drunkenness.
conn.: negative.
con.st.i.: The Dutch are greedy and have bad manners.

Dutch nickel 'a kiss.'

fig.d.:	metaphor.
sem.f.:	love.
conn.:	slightly negative.
con.st.i.:	The Dutch are stereotyped as thieves. Thus, such a kiss has been stolen. (cf. Green)

Dutch nightingale 'a frog.'

fig.d.:	antiphrasis.
sem.f.:	animals.
conn.:	ironic.
con.st.i.:	cf. *Dutch concert/ medley*.

Dutch reckoning 1. 'a bill presented as a lump sum with no details attached.'
2. 'a bad day's work.'

fig.d.:	metonymy.
sem.f.:	money, business.
conn.:	negative.
con.st.i.:	cf. *Dutch auction*.

Dutch rub 'to rub one's knuckles hard across one's victims skull.'

fig.d.:	metonymy.
sem.f.:	physical violence.
conn.:	negative.
con.st.i.:	The Dutch are violent and gruff.

Dutch treat/ lunch/ party/ supper 'an outing, a visit to a restaurant etc. in which the costs are shared equally, i.e. there is no 'treat' at all in the sense of one party being entertained at the other's expense.'
fig.d.: antiphrasis.
sem.f.: meanness.
conn.: sarcastic.
con.st.i.: cf. *Dutch fuck.*

Dutch uncle 'one who talks severely and critically, who lays down the law.'
fig.d.: metonymy.
sem.f.: personality traits.
conn.: derogative.
con.st.i.: cf. *dutch.*

5.4.1 General Analysis

The most terms, namely 24 percent, are from the semantic field of *money and business*. The implied stereotype is that of the malicious and mercenary Dutch that must not be trusted in business affairs. According to Green, the negative stereotype of the Dutch originates from the 17th century when the English fought the Dutch as a national enemy (cf. Green, p. 382). Although, this stereotype is not as current as it used to be back then, there are still expressions in use which imply that particular national stereotype (e.g. *Dutch treat/ lunch/ party/ supper*). That circumstance well illustrates how long-lived and extremely resistible to change certain stereotypes are.

The Dutch are furthermore stereotyped as miserly, bossy, quick-tempered and having a natural inclination to drink large quantities of alcohol (19 percent of the terms are from the semantic field of *alcohol and drunkenness*). Just like the slang terms implying Irish stereotypes, most of the listed expressions have a derogative or negative connotation.

5.5 Slang Terms Containing Jewish Stereotypes

jew/ jew down/ up 'to cheat financially.'
fig.d.: metonymy.
sem.f.: money, business.
conn.: negative.
con.st.i.: Jewish businessmen are cheaters and thus not to be trusted.

Jew canoe 'a Jaguar.'
fig.d.: metaphor, dysphemism.
sem.f.: luxury.
conn.: derogative.
con.st.i.: Jews show off with expensive cars. A jaguar is a typically Jewish status symbol.

Jew cheque 'any form of cheque that is obtained through fraud, e.g. on Social Security.'
fig.d.: metonymy, sarcasm.
sem.f.: fraud.
conn.: negative.
con.st.i.: Jews are cheaters and not to be trusted.

Jewish airlines 'walking.'

fig.d.: irony.
sem.f.: movement.
conn.: ironic.
con.st.i.: Jews are too mean to spend any money on means of transport.

Jewish/ Jew flag 'a currency note.'

fig.d.: metaphor.
sem.f.: money, business.
conn.: negative.
con.st.i.: Jews are obsessed with making money and everything that has got to do with it.

Jewish foreplay 'the man pleads for sex, his partner refuses all physical contact.'

fig.d.: antiphrasis, sarcasm.
sem.f.: sexuality.
conn.: sarcastic.
con.st.i.: Jewish women are frigid and their husbands are lousy sexual performers.

Jewish lightening 'deliberate arson in order to gain insurance on an otherwise unprofitable business.'

fig.d.: metaphor, irony.
sem.f.: fraud.
conn.: negative.
con.st.i.: cf. *Jewish cheque*.

Jewish overdrive 'freewheeling down hills to save petrol.'	
fig.d.: metaphor.	
sem.f.: meanness.	
conn.: ironic.	
con.st.i.: Jews are mean.	

Jewish piano 'a cash register.'	
fig.d.: metaphor, irony.	
sem.f.: money, business.	
conn.: slightly negative.	
con.st.i.: cf. *Jewish/ Jew flag*.	

Jewish prince 'a Jewish man who is spoiled or dominated by his mother.'	
fig.d.: metaphor, irony.	
sem.f.: personality traits.	
conn.: derogative.	
con.st.i.: Jewish men are spoiled when young and remain dominated by their mothers.	

Jewish princess 'young, conceited (middle-class) Jewish woman.'	
fig.d.: metaphor, irony.	
sem.f.: personality traits.	
conn.: derogative.	
con.st.i.: Conceitedness of new-rich Jewish women.	

Jewish screwdriver 'a hammer.'

fig.d.: antiphrasis, sarcasm.
sem.f.: tools.
conn.: sarcastic.
con.st.i.: Jews are too stupid and clumsy to use tools properly and perform simple manual tasks. (cf. *French screwdriver* and *Irish screwdriver*.)

Jewish sidewalls 'white rubber sidewalls, glued onto otherwise black tyres in an attempt to make them look more fashionable.'

fig.d.: metonymy.
sem.f.: motorised vehicles.
conn.: negative.
con.st.i.: cf. *Jewish overdrive*.

Jewish time/ standard time 'unpunctuality time.'

fig.d.: metonymy, irony.
sem.f.: time.
conn.: negative.
con.st.i.: Jews arrive late for any meeting or appointments.

Jewish typewriter 'a cash register.'

fig.d.: metaphor, irony.
sem.f.: money, business.
conn.: slightly negative.
con.st.i.: cf. *Jewish piano*.

Jewish waltz 'deal-making, haggling.'

fig.d.: metaphor, irony.	
sem.f.: money, business.	
conn.: negative.	
con.st.i.: cf. *Jewish flag*. Making business is an essential pleasure to Jews, just as dancing is to others.	

Jewman 'a moneylender.'

fig.d.: metonymy.	
sem.f.: money, business.	
conn.: negative.	
con.st.i.: The 'profession' of the moneylender is typically Jewish.	

Jew's balls 'a pawnbroker.'

fig.d.: metonymy.	
sem.f.: money, business.	
conn.: slightly negative.	
con.st.i.: The profession of the pawnbroker is also typically Jewish.	

Jew's/ Jewish compliment 'a large penis but no money or presents.'

fig.d.: schematismus, irony.	
sem.f.: sexuality	
conn.: sarcastic.	
con.st.i.: Jews are mean. The penis is free but presents would involve losing money. (cf. Green)	

Jew shave 'covering one's face with talcum powder instead of shaving.'

fig.d.: irony.
sem.f.: hygiene.
conn.: derogative.
con.st.i.: Jews are mean, untidy and dirty.

Jew York 'New York.'

fig.d.: pun, allusion.
sem.f.: city names.
conn.: negative.
con.st.i.: Allusion to the large Jewish population of New York. Jews allegedly control the city, especially the financial business.

5.5.1 General Analysis

Strictly speaking, the common stereotype of Jews is a racial rather than a national one. However, it is certainly one of the most interesting to investigate. According to the results from Katz's and Braly's study, Jews are primarily stereotyped as 'shrewd' and 'mercenary' (cf. Chapter 3.4.1). This stereotype has been widely spread in Europe since the Middle Ages. Green observes that "in slang, reflecting centuries of Christian teaching, the Jew is grasping, avaricious, wealthy, untrustworthy, deceitful and mean" (Green, p. 661). 29 percent of the expressions are from the semantic field of *money and business*. They all imply that Jews are duplicitous businessmen that are obsessed with money and must not be trusted. The key result is that the Jewish stereotype in slang is practically the same one as in Katz's and Braly's study.

As it has already been mentioned, one of the primary functions of slang is to put down 'the others' that do not belong to the speakers group or community. Actually, all of the terms listed are derogative and play on the common stereotype of the Jew. Contrary to most of the 'Dutch' slang terms, the listed expressions are still current, especially in the United States. Thus, it can be assumed that the Jewish stereotype is probably the most enduring racial stereotype ever.

5.6 Slang Terms Containing German Stereotypes

German 'a sausage, a wurst.'
fig.d.: metonymy.
sem.f.: food.
conn.: neutral.
con.st.i.: Germans eat large quantities of wurst.

German aunt 'a fat, frumpish woman.'
fig.d.: metonymy, sarcasm.
sem.f.: derogative terms for women.
conn.: derogative.
con.st.i.: German women are fat and untidy. (cf. *French aunt*.)

German comb 'the hand.'
fig.d.: metaphor, irony.
sem.f.: hygiene.
conn.: derogative.
con.st.i.: Germans are untidy and lack sophistication.

German duck 'a bedbug.'
fig.d.: metaphor.
sem.f.: hygiene.
conn.: negative.
con.st.i.: Germans are dirty and untidy.

German goitre 'a beer belly, a noticeable paunch.'
fig.d.: metaphor, dysphemism.
sem.f.: appearance.
conn.: derogative.
con.st.i.: Germans drink large quantities of beer and have an enormous capacity for it.

German helmet 'the glans penis.'
fig.d.: metaphor.
sem.f.: sexuality.
conn.: neutral.
con.st.i.: The form of the glans penis resembles a military helmet. Germans are typically associated with anything that has got to do with the military.

German marching pills 'amphetamines, esp. Methedrine, a German invention.'
fig.d.: metaphor.
sem.f.: drugs and narcotics.
conn.: negative.
con.st.i.: see *German helmet*.

German silver 'anything that is sham, fake.'
fig.d.: metonymy, irony.
sem.f.: fraud.
conn.: negative.
con.st.i.: Germans are deceitful and thus not to be trusted.

5.6.1 General Analysis

In the case of German stereotypes in slang it is quite difficult to make a clear statement since there is no obvious result that can be worked out, due to the relatively small number of expressions that exist or rather were recorded and found their way into dictionaries.

However, it could be argued that the slang terms listed imply that the stereotypical German has a large capacity for beer, is untrustworthy and lacks sophistication and proper hygiene. That stereotype is rather contrary to the one in Katz and Braly's study that emphasises other qualities such as 'scientifically-minded' and 'intelligent' for instance (cf. Chapter 3.4.1).

5.7 Slang Terms Containing English Stereotypes

English 'sadomasochistic.'
fig.d.: metonomy, camouflage.
sem.f.: sexuality.
conn.: derogative.
con.st.i.: The English have sadomasochistic tendencies.

English bearer 'a drunken man with a red face.'
fig.d.: metaphor.
sem.f.: alcohol and drunkenness.
conn.: ironic.
con.st.i.: The English consume a lot of alcohol and thus have red faces.

English cold/ winter 'iced tea.'
fig.d.: metaphor.
sem.f.: beverages.
conn.: neutral.
con.st.i.: Tea is something quintessentially English.

English culture 'sex advertisements for bondage and discipline.'
fig.d.: antiphrasis, sarcasm.
sem.f.: sexuality.
conn.: sarcastic.
con.st.i.: The English enjoy unusual sexual practices; are sadomasochistic and sexually neurotic.

English disease 1. 'melancholy.'   2. 'rickets.'   3. 'a propensity for industrial action and strikes.'   4. 'erotic flagellation.'

fig.d.: 1., 2., and 3. metonymy.   4. dysphemism.
sem.f.: 1. and 2. diseases   3. work   4. sexuality
conn.: 1. and 2. negative.   3. and 4. derogative.
con.st.i.: 1. The English generally are a melancholic people.   2. The English are (used to be) a sick people because of their bad nutrition.   3. The English are bad and constantly malcontent workers, employees.   4. cf. *English culture*.

English guidance 'bondage and discipline.'

fig.d.: metonymy, euphemism.
sem.f.: sexuality.
conn.: ironic.
con.st.i.: cf. *English culture*.

Englishified 'said of one who has returned from a stay in England with an English accent and generally more sophisticated.'

fig.d.: metonymy.
sem.f.: personality traits.
conn.: derogative.
con.st.i.: Alleged sophistication and conceitedness of the English.

English martini 'tea; especially when spiked with gin.'

fig.d.: metaphor, irony.
sem.f.: beverages.
conn.: neutral.
con.st.i.: English people spike all their beverages with alcohol.

English method 'intercrural homosexual intercourse, i.e. non-penetrative rubbing between closed thighs.'

fig.d.: metonymy, camouflage.
sem.f.: sexuality.
conn.: derogative.
con.st.i.: English homosexuals are sexually inhibited.

English sentry 'the erect penis.'

fig.d.: metaphor.
sem.f.: sexuality.
conn.: ironic.
con.st.i.: Alleged reputation of the English Guardsmen for gay prostitution. (cf. Green)

English sunbathing 'sitting fully-clothed in the sun.'

fig.d.: irony.
sem.f.: leisure time activities.
conn.: ironic.
con.st.i.: The English are too foolish to enjoy the sun since it never shines in their country.

5.7.1 General Analysis

The most striking and interesting aspect is that no less than 55 percent of the terms containing stereotypes of the English are from the semantic field of *sexuality*. The results from the analysis are significantly different to those from Katz's and Braly's study in which the English are primarily characterised as 'sportsmanlike', 'intelligent' and 'conventional' (cf. Chapter 3.4.1). The stereotypical Englishman in slang is sadomasochistic, particularly fond of 'queer' sexual practices, especially bondage, and might thus be considered sexually neurotic. This sharp contrast between the two results may be due to the fact that slang often circles around social taboos such as certain aspects of sexuality as it is the case here. The Katz and Braly study on the other hand was carried out in a rather formal context and thus almost exclusively neglects the field of sexuality.

6 CONCLUSION AND OUTLOOK

National stereotyping in slang has proved to be a complex subject, that can be approached from different angles and includes a great variety of interesting aspects. Thus, to achieve a comprehensive understanding of the subject, it has been necessary to provide a well-founded theoretical treatment of the fields of stereotyping and slang, as well as to investigate their interrelation.

Stereotyping manifests itself predominantly through language. This basic assumption has been proved and illustrated in the course of this paper. Furthermore, it has been worked out that slang, due to its particular characteristics and functions, is an ideal linguistic means to convey stereotypes. The vocabulary of slang provides an enormous number of expressions that imply national stereotypes. Only a small part of those expressions has been analysed within the survey in Chapter 5, due to the given length of such a paper as this one. The survey, however, has mainly been supposed to fulfil an exemplary function rather than a representative one.

Furthermore, there are certain aspects that could not be discussed, for a comprehensive treatment of them would have gone beyond the scope of this paper's topic focus. However, it would be very interesting for instance, to investigate when and why certain national stereotypes came into being, with paying particular attention to the historic relations between selected nations. There certainly lies great potential for further research within this field.

7 BIBLIOGRAPHY

Primary Sources:
- Ayton, John, ed. *The Oxford Dictionary of Modern Slang*. Oxford: Oxford University Press, 2005.
- Burgess, Anthony. *A Clockwork Orange*. London: Penguin Books, 1998.
- "fag." *The Collins German Dictionary: Unabridged*. 4th ed. 1980.
- "fag." *The Concise Oxford Dictionary*. 9th ed. 1996.
- Green, Jonathon, ed. *The Cassell's Dictionary of Slang*. London: Cassell, 2000.
- "List of common phrases based on stereotypes." *Wikipedia*. Wikipedia, 2005. Answers.com GuruNet Corp. 02 Sep. 2005. http://www.answers.com/topic/list-of-common-phrases-based-on-stereotypes
- Orwell, George. "Notes on Nationalism." *The Collected Essays, Journalism and Letters of George Orwell*. Ed. Sonja Orwell. London: Secker and Warburg, 1968.
- "slang." *The Oxford English Dictionary*. 2nd ed. 1989.
- Spears, Richard, ed. *Slang and Euphemism*. 3rd ed. New York: Signet 2001.
- "taboo." *The Concise Oxford Dictionary*. 9th ed. 1996.
- Thorne, Toney, ed. *The Dictionary of Contemporary Slang*. New York: Pantheon Books, 1999.

Secondary Sources:
- Anderson, Lars-Gunar, and Peter Trudgill. *Bad Language*. London: Penguin Books, 1992.
- Bering, Jan, and Christiane Villain-Gandossi. "The Role and Significance of National Stereotypes in International Relations: An Interdisciplinary Approach." *Stereotypes and Nations*. Ed. Theresa Walas. Krakow: Drukarnia UJ, 1995.
- Brown, Robert. *Social Psychology*. London: Collier-Macmillan, 1965.
- Burchfield, Robert. *The English Language*. Oxford: Oxford University Press, 2002.
- Burgess, Anthony. *A Mouthful of Air*. London: Vintage, 1993.

- Crystal, David. *The Cambridge Encyclopaedia of the English Language.* Cambridge: Cambridge University Press, 1995.
- Fox, Robyn. "Prejudice and the Unfinished Mind: A New Look on an Old Failing." *Psychological Inquiry* 3 (1992): 137-152.
- "General Explanations." *The Oxford English Dictionary.* 2nd ed. 1989.
- Hamilton, David L., and Tina K. Troiler. "Stereotypes and Stereotyping: An Overview of the Cognitive Approach." *Prejudice, Discrimination and Racism.* Ed. John F. Dovido. Orlando: Academic Press, 1986.
- Hinton, Perry. *Stereotypes, Cognition and Culture.* Philadelphia: Taylor and Francis, 2000.
- Jackson, Howard. *Words, Meaning and Vocabulary.* London: Continuum, 2001.
- Katamba, Francis. English *Words: Structure, History and Usage.* 2nd ed. New York: Routledge, 2005.
- Katz, Daniel, and Kenneth Braly. "Racial Stereotypes in One Hundred College Students." *Journal of Abnormal and Social Psychology.* 28 (1933): 280-290.
- van Langenhove, Luk, and Rom Harré. "Cultural Stereotypes and Positioning Theory." *Journal of Personality and Social Psychology.* 45 (1994): 961-977.
- Leisi, Ernst, and Christian Mair. *Das Heutige Englisch: Wesenszüge und Probleme.* 8th ed. Heidelberg: Universitätsverlag C. Winter, 1999.
- Lighter, Jonathan. "Slang." *The Cambridge History of the English Language.* Ed. John Algeo. Vol. 6. Cambridge: Cambridge University Press, 2001.
- Lippmann, Walter. *Public Opinion.* New York: Macmillan, 1922.
- "List of common stereotypes based on nationality, ethnicity and race." *Wikipedia.* Wikipedia, 2005. Answers.com GuruNet Corp. 02 Sep. 2005. http://en.wikipedia.org/wiki/User:Grue/List_of_ethnic_stereotypes
- Löschmann, Martin. "Stereotype, Stereotype und Kein Ende." *Stereotype im Fremdsprachenunterricht.* Eds. Martin Löschmann und Magda Stroinska. Frankfurt am Main: Lang, 1998.

- Maas, Anne. "Language Use in Intergroup Contexts: The Linguistic Intergroup Bias." *Journal of Personality and Social Psychology.* 67 (1989): 981-993.
- Maas, Anne, and Luciano Arcuri. "Language and Stereotyping." *Stereotypes and Stereotyping.* Eds. C. Neil Macrae, Charles Stangor and Miles Hewstone. London: The Guilford Press, 1996.
- Meyer, Paul G. *Synchronic English Linguistics.* Tübingen: Gunter Narr Verlag, 2002.
- "nation." *Wikipedia.* Wikipedia, 2005. Answers.com GuruNet Corp. 26 Aug. 2005. http://www.answers.com/topic/nation-2
- Partridge, Eric. *Slang: Today and Yesterday.* 4th ed. London: Routledge, 1972.
- Putnam, Hilary. *Die Bedeutung von Bedeutung.* Trans. Wolfgang Spohn. Frankfurt am Main: Klostermann, 1979.
- Quasthoff, Uta. *Soziales Vorurteil und Kommunikation: Eine Sprachwissenschaftliche Analyse des Stereotyps.* Frankfurt am Main: Athenäum-Fischer, 1973.
- "schematismus." *Silva Rhetoricae.* Online Rethoric, 2005. Dr. Gideon Burton of Brigham Young University. 02 Sep. 2005. http://humanities.byu.edu/rhetoric/Figures/S/schematismus.htm
- Sodi, Kripal Singh, and Rudolf Bergius. "Nationale Vorurteile." *Forschungen zur Sozialpsychologie und Ethnologie.* Band 1. Ed. Robert Thurnwald. Berlin: Duncker & Humblot, 1953.
- "stereotype." *Wikipedia.* Wikipedia, 2005. Answers.com GuruNet Corp. 22 Aug. 2005. http://www.answers.com/topic/stereotype
- Stockwell, Peter. *Sociolinguistics.* London: Routledge, 2002.
- Stroinska, Magda. "Them and Us: On Cognitive and Pedagogical Aspects of Language Based Stereotyping." *Stereotype im Fremdsprachenunterricht.* Eds. Martin Löschmann and Magda Stroinska. Frankfurt am Main: Lang, 1998.
- *The Oxford Companion to the English Language.* Ed. Tom McArthur. Oxford: Oxford University Press, 1992.
- Walas, Teresa, ed. *Stereotypes and Nations.* Krakow: Drukarnia UJ, 1995.

- Zybatow, Lew. *Russisch im Wandel: Die Russische Sprache Seit der Perestrojka*. Wiesbaden: Harrassowitz, 1995.

***ibidem*-Verlag**
Melchiorstr. 15
D-70439 Stuttgart

info@ibidem-verlag.de

www.ibidem-verlag.de
www.edition-noema.de
www.autorenbetreuung.de

www.ingramcontent.com/pod-product-compliance
Lightning Source LLC
Chambersburg PA
CBHW060343170426
43202CB00014B/2860